GARDENS

by Peter Shepheard BArch FRIBA AMTPI FILA

A Design Centre Publication

Peter Shepheard

Macdonald & Co (Publishers) Ltd in association with the Council of Industrial Design 1969

Ana D. Thompson
October 1975

Contents

A landing place in one of the gardens of the old Imperial Palace, Kyoto, where a few stones, a few plants and some water recreate a natural landscape in a few square yards

Introduction

Almost everyone who plans a garden will agree that beauty is what he is after; and yet, of all the thousands of books on gardening, very few attempt to specify what makes a garden beautiful. This little book tries to do this. Its subject is not so much the technique of gardening—though that must come into it—as how the technique affects the beauty of the result. The technique in this sense is not only that of growing plants; the beauty of a garden depends just as much, if not even more, on the hard stuff such as paving, walls and fences, and on the arrangement and planning of the available space.

House and Garden

First, a garden is an extension of a house. The life that goes on in the house should be able to spread into the garden, as if it were a large and somewhat less private living room. The design of the house itself should make this possible—the main living room should open on to the garden, if possible with french windows, and a paved terrace for outdoor meals. Too often this is made impossible by the arrangement of the house itself; instead of french windows one finds casements with a cill high enough to obstruct the view of the garden from a sitting position; or where there could be a terrace, with wing walls for privacy, there may be sheds and dustbins. Such defects call for adjustment or camouflage: make a new window, or rearrange the dustbins and sheds, or screen them with climbing plants.

Ideally, even the smallest garden should offer some privacy in the open air; at least a place where one could have an outdoor meal, immediately outside the living room, on a paved terrace, with wing walls at least 5′ 6″ high running out from the house a little way to give enclosure from the neighbours. Sometimes a part of the house or garage can form this dividing screen.

A very pleasant arrangement is for each house to have a private terrace or patio of this sort, giving on to a small rectangle of garden, which in turn has a gate into a common garden shared between two rows of houses. This provides a gradation of privacy—terrace almost as private as indoors, garden semi-private, and common garden where one meets the neighbours. If this common garden is mainly grass and trees, and if the neighbours join in its upkeep, it makes an ideal playground, away from roads, where the children of the group of houses can meet and play. With such a layout, and with good planning of the houses and their garages and dustbin arrangements, one of the most urgent problems of garden planning—how to cater for the various *uses* of the garden in the small space usually available—is solved at the start; there is space already made for eating out, sitting in the sun, growing plants, childrens' play and so on.

Usually, however, one is faced with a given plot, of which the shape,

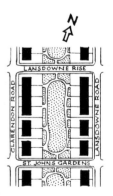

The arrangement of the common gardens in the Lansdowne Road area of London

The common garden: small
private gardens, giving on to a
common garden shared by all;
in Lansdowne Road, London,
about 1850

Private garden designed by
Derek Bridgwater.

Photographs: Derek Bridgwater

aspect and soil are all more or less matters of chance, and much of the success of gardening on such a site comes from sensing its limitations and advantages and making suitable plans. There is almost no site, however small, however shaded, or however barren the soil, on which a work of garden art cannot be created; but you have to work with what's there, and turn even the slenderest advantages to good account.

The Basic Elements

Soil

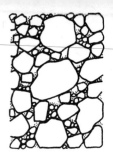

Particles of a sandy soil. Sandgrains (2–.02 mm dia) with finer silt (.02–.002 mm dia) and clay (.002 or less)

All plants need topsoil to grow in. Topsoil is the precious thin layer of darker soil, containing humus and bacteria, which lies over the subsoils of the world to a depth of a few inches to a few feet. Subsoil is rock, weathered into small particles. The topsoil is formed over thousands of years, mainly by the action of earthworms which drag down dead vegetation and other organic material (humus) into the earth and mix it with the subsoil matrix. This mixture contains a vast number of microscopic animals and bacteria; these feed on the humus and convert it into plant food.

The plant obtains the food elements dissolved in water which is sucked up by the roots. The water forms a film on the surfaces of the soil particles with air spaces between them; this air is needed for the survival of the bacteria and the growth of the roots. When there is so much water that it fills the spaces between the soil particles, the soil is 'waterlogged'; if this condition persists, the bacteria and the plants die. Normally, the water drains to deeper levels, drawing air in behind it and leaving the particle surfaces moist.

On this topsoil, thus drained, all plant life depends. It can be easily lost or destroyed during building operations; it should first be removed and stacked and only replaced after building is finished. If the topsoil from a house site is spread over the garden, one should end up with a considerably deeper layer. Too often it is lost, mixed with subsoil, buried, or simply stolen from the site—it is valuable and can be sold for up to £3 per cubic yard. Moreover, machines pounding the subsoil, especially clay, in wet weather can puddle it to form a hard impervious 'pan' which will prevent drainage of the topsoil when it is replaced and produce a waterlogged layer in which nothing will grow. The only remedy for this is deep digging and breaking up of the pan, and restoration of the drainage; it may never again be as good as the virgin ground, and may need land drains to take surplus water away.

Heavy and light soils
Because the water is held as a film on the surface of the soil particles, the *size* of the particles determines both the amount that can be held and the speed with which it drains away. The surface area of fine particles in a given bulk is much greater than that of coarse particles— clay particles may have a surface area 10 to 15 times that of coarse sand

Opposite:
A favoured site: light soil, south aspect, sheltering walls east and west, with a wonderful view— in which Frederick MacManus has created a rich little garden. Rye, Sussex

6

particles; clay soils therefore hold far more water, and retain it longer than sands; they are known as 'heavy' soils, while sands are dry and 'light'. Extremely fine clays are stiff and difficult to dig, but they can be very fertile; extremely coarse sands are loose and easy to dig, but can be arid and barren. One can find some species of plants adapted to thrive in each of the extremes; but the ideal garden soil, which will grow a large *variety* of plants, is one of medium or mixed particle size— a good 'loam' as gardeners say.

Humus is also very retentive of water, and both heavy and light soils are improved by adding more of it. In heavy soils it loosens the texture and helps to admit air; in light soils it enriches the texture and helps to retain moisture. Light soils are usually lacking in humus; moreover, because water drains through them rapidly, plant foods are more quickly washed out, or 'leached' into the subsoil, so that light soils are always improved by extra organic material.

Acid and alkaline soils

Some soils are naturally acid, some alkaline; and some plants are adapted to grow solely in one or the other. There is, however, a continuous gradation from one extreme to the other, and the middling 'neutral' soils grow the widest range of species. The range is measured by the hydrogen-ion concentration, and expressed by a negative logarithm called a pH value, the low numbers acid, the high alkaline: an acid peat moor might give pH3; pH7 is neutral, pH8 is alkaline, and would contain free calcium carbonate. For gardeners, the main disadvantage of an alkaline soil is that it will not grow certain plants such as Rhododendrons and Ericas, and that an abundance of calcium hastens the decomposition of organic material to such an extent that the soil may need heavy manuring. Most plants prefer a soil just on the acid side of neutral; and it is easy to cure extreme acidity in a small garden by judicious addition of lime. However, there are beautiful plants for all types of soil—even a few species of Rhododendron and Erica which will tolerate chalk—and the first principle of gardening is to have plants which like your soil and thrive in it.

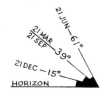

Angle of sun at noon, lat 51°

Sun and Shade

The aspect of the house and garden will decide many things for you. A south-west aspect for the living room will have sun in the window from about 9.30 am till sundown; the terrace will be sunny for all meals except early breakfast; you will see your garden, from the living room, with a side light in the morning, and against the sun in the afternoon and evening. I find this delightful; many plants benefit from this back lighting by the sun—leaves glisten and shine, flowers glow against the shadows cast by other plants. If the house does not face south-west, you may have to move the terrace into the sun, and make other calculations about how the light falls on your garden. But always, in this climate, the sunlight is precious, both to sit in and to illuminate

The rings show the duration of daylight at the solstices and the equinoxes, lat 51°

The texture of young chestnut
leaves lit from behind by the
sun. This capacity of trees to hold
sunlight is an essential factor in
placing them in the garden

Seen against the sun, the leaves of
Rodgersia and Osmunda both hold
and reflect light

your garden; and the way the sunlight falls is a major factor in the placing of each element in the garden design, both plants and structures. It is of absolutely paramount importance when designing ponds and fountains.

While sun is good, especially to sit in, the whole garden need not bask in it. Some gardeners who find themselves with a partly shaded garden will fret unduly about lack of sun, and even cut down fine trees to let in more sun to beds of flowers. Often the deep shade of a great tree or building can be made a key element in the design, by arranging plants to be sunlit against the shade, and filling the shade itself with some of the vast army of beautiful shade-loving plants. Indeed, a uniformly sunlit garden is dull, and will always benefit by the contrast of deep shade.

Shelter

In our climate, shutting out the wind from a plot of ground has the same effect as moving it five hundred miles farther south. This was well known to the mediaeval builders, who always grouped buildings round courts and cloisters, and there are many existing examples of old kitchen gardens sheltered by 10 ft walls on which grow peaches and other southern plants.

Wind is an enemy of plants, not only because it knocks them about, but also because it desiccates them by increasing the rate of transpiration of water from their leaves. In Britain strong winds often occur in the spring when newly opened leaves are particularly tender. Even a 6 ft wall will provide useful wind shelter, both for plants and people, and considerable slowing down of wind is found in the lee of more open fences such as bamboo, chestnut paling, or even wire netting; indeed, against very strong winds partly-open screens such as plantations are better than solid ones which cause turbulence on the lee side. It is important that enclosures made by buildings or solid walls should be *complete*; to leave gaps is to admit draughts which are accelerated by the enclosure of the rest. The higher sheltering elements, whether walls, buildings or tree screens, should be on the north, and lower screens round the other sides to let the slanting sun come over them. Solid walls and screens are expensive, but very useful for carrying climbers and wall plants.

Near the coast and some miles inland, especially in the west, the salt-laden sea winds are particularly destructive to plants; gardens in such areas, however, are often fairly free from frost and, as soon as they are sheltered by screens made of the few plants which will resist salt winds, they will grow many plants which would be killed by cold in inland areas; a splendid example is at Abbotsbury in Dorset.

Campanula Latifolia, a graceful white flowered plant, seen against the shade of trees at Wisley

Planning

Planning is merely making carefully considered decisions before action. It enables you to do more with a given space than is possible by muddling through. Few gardens have enough room for all the things a family wants to do; but the first step is to decide *what* it wants to do, now and in the future, and then to try to arrange for as many activities as possible without their clashing with each other.

A garden merely for walking and sitting in presents few problems; but even sitting needs privacy and shelter from wind.

Eating out
Needs a paved terrace, fairly smooth for chairs, from which crumbs can be swept, near the kitchen and living room, with lighting for use after dark.

Parties
Need a fairly smooth area. A grass lawn will do, especially if large, for fine weather; but grass is unusable for hours after rain, and paving is better, with seats and tables or slabs for putting things down on.

Children
Are the main beneficiaries of the garden. In a small garden, while the children are very young, horticulture must take second place to their needs. But they grow up quickly; from their earliest exploratory stage —when the plants suffer most but the children learn most—they soon become responsible and even interested; soon afterwards they leave the garden for ever. So the early installations should be designed with the future in mind—sand pit can become flowerbed; paddling pool, lily pond; and so on.

The look of the thing

Architecture has been called the interplay of masses in light and shade; this is as true of gardens. It is the light of the sun, reflected from the surfaces of every object in the garden, that renders the garden visible. All forms, textures and colours are simply reflected light; as the light fails in the evening, they gradually sink from sight and in the dark they have gone.

A garden designer—like an architect or a sculptor—must regard light as his medium. And, whereas the hard materials of a building reflect light in a regular and easily predictable way, many of the elements of a garden—plants, for example, and water—are much more subtle. The complex leafy structure of a plant is full of shade, and plants generally appear darker than the hard surfaces of paving and walls; but some plants have large shiny leaves which glisten in the sun making silvery lights against the shade. Most flowers and young leaves have a thin translucent texture which the sun can shine through; when seen against the sun, with a background of shadow, they can be dazzling bright.

Good gardens are made by those who notice such things; some say, who have a *feeling*; but it is really all observation and love.

An essential quality of the light of this country is of course the lowness of the sun and the frequency of cloud, mist and haze. This is probably one of the reasons why our architecture has a tradition of ornament, pattern and silhouette instead of the hard clear forms cut by the Mediterranean sun. But this gentle light paradoxically increases the brilliance of colours, which the southern sun tends to diminish; even the purple heather and the red-brown bracken have a deep brilliance under an English sky, and the ubiquitous grass is a truly violent colour.

Children need gardens: when
young to mess about in, and
when older for games and social
life

This means that it is quite easy to overdo colour in English gardens, and it is always a puzzle why a 'riot of colour' is so often used as a term of praise.

Perspective

Although a plan is needed as a guide to the work, it gives a poor idea of what a garden will look like except from an aeroplane. But a garden is usually seen from *eye level*—5 ft standing and 4 ft sitting; heights are therefore far more important than length and width. A fence 4 ft high cuts off a lot of ground from view; make it 5' 6" and it cuts off *everything*. From eye level slight curves in a path become acute bends, square patterns in paving collapse and become narrow diamonds, and the trees which look like green cushions on a plan rear themselves far into the air and allow distant views underneath them. This effect of perspective, which causes all the objects in a garden to be seen one behind the other, with complicated overlappings and obstructions, calls for designing in three dimensions. Somehow, one must *visualise* how it will appear to the eye—either by drawing sketches or by marking out the site with sticks and stones and string.

Perspective can be put to work to overcome the disadvantages of a site. A long narrow plot can be made to seem broader by a repetition of lines running across it; a distance can be made to seem greater by lines running away from the eye; a path can be made to seem longer by a slight tapering of its width—but this works one way only and it will look *shorter* from the other end!

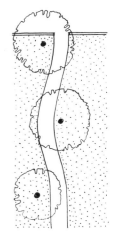

Levels

Few garden plots are absolutely level. Even on the gentlest slopes one can, by a modest amount of earth-moving, make steps or slight drops in level which will define different parts of the garden. If a plot is absolutely level, one can still remove 6 in. of soil from a large area—say a lawn—and add it to a smaller area of terrace or beds to make say a 1' 6" step; beds thus raised will grow plants better because they will have better drainage and deeper topsoil.

Traditions and the Source of Ideas

Anyone designing a garden brings to it his own ideas of what a garden should be. Too often these seem to stem from a sentimental preconception, summed up for me in that dreadful verse which begins 'a garden is a lovesome thing, God wot'. The mode consists of a very strange collection of elements which have an outrageous incongruity with each other and with all modern situations: Cotswold stone retaining walls; vaguely Spanish wrought-iron gates; 'crazy' paving, nowadays often coloured yellow, green and pink; tiny irregular ponds, now usually of pale blue fibreglass, fed by streams of improbable

Perspective: gentle curves on a plan become sharp bends in perspective. Trees coalesce above but allow views beneath their branches. A 6 ft fence stops the view entirely

The designer's
medium is light,
which renders the
world visible.

Geneva in rain and
sunshine

Beaulieu river in mist and morning light

Cyprus in sun and sinking into night

source; gnomes, fairies and animals, usually plastic, of vaguely Neapolitan colouring; dwarf Cypress trees. The list is longer, but enough: in short, 'Godwottery' beautifully proves the truth of a definition (by V. S. Pritchett, I think) of sentimentality in art as 'having the idea of the feeling before the feeling'.

The remedy is to shun preconceptions, observe nature, and above all trust one's own feeling for the stuff of which the landscape is made. In the study of the wild landscape itself—and indeed of much of the man-made landscape—one finds lessons about the growth of plants, the movement of water, the structure of rocks and sea shores, all of which in some mysterious way have relevance to the design of gardens, even if only as part of an underlying comprehension of the way nature works. Gertrude Jekyll's books, especially *Wood and Garden*, are a perfect example; they are full of references to her delight in the countryside, and of country crafts and cottage gardens, and of her direct use of this knowledge and affection in her work. More lessons can be learnt from the towns, villages, harbours and canals of the country, especially those built in the age of craftsmen; here one finds paving and steps, walls and fences, kerbs and gutters—a thousand problems solved in permanent and beautiful forms.

Finally, there are the great national traditions of garden design which present an inexhaustible treasure-house of forms and ideas. Many garden designers have fingered through this vast store, and picked up a motif here and there, sticking them into their work as concrete proof of their lack of understanding. History cannot be used in this way. But each of the great traditions is rooted in the local climate and landscape and based on the architecture, craftsmanship and way of life of the people. Consider, for example, the Italian, the Moorish and the Japanese gardens. The Italian tradition is a product of the renaissance, and boldly imposes human values on the landscape; the gardens are big, for crowds, parties and display; the site and its vegetation are brilliantly manipulated and decorated with sophisticated architecture in a classical mode; water is thrown about and made to perform spectacular tricks. The Moorish tradition is in utter contrast; even the great palace gardens of Seville and Granada are divided into small walled enclosures, for the private enjoyment of one man and his wives; the precious water is led down from a tiny source through court after court, in slender fountains and rivulets which sing of coolness— these immensely subtle and delicious gardens are paradises, oases in an arid land. The Japanese tradition, remote and esoteric, and difficult to appreciate without knowledge of its religious and cultural background, has nevertheless been favourite copy for English gardeners, usually with disastrous results. For the true message of Japanese gardens is that you cannot *copy* nature, but if you love nature enough you can create gardens which can compress the wonder of a whole landscape into a few square yards, with nothing but a few stones, a few plants and some sand.

Above: a lychgate
in the Cotswolds
shows the simple
English tradition of
country landscape,
based on grass, trees
and craftsmanship
in stone and wood
Right: its exact
opposite: high
"Godwottery"

17

A garden is an artefact made in collaboration with nature. It is essential to remember the contrast between the artificial conditions of the garden and the natural conditions of the heath, the bog or the forest. In nature, plants and trees, and indeed all living things, grow together as parts of a balanced scheme; in a garden this ecological balance is erased, and in its place stands the gardener. He must hold the balance, and the more he knows about the way plants grow and live together, the better will his garden grow.

The Elements

The elements of garden work fall into two categories: the hard—building constructions, paving, walls, ponds, etc; and the soft—vegetation and the soil it grows in. While there are thousands of books on the soft, it is very difficult to find books which give reliable advice on the hard. Plenty of books of course deal with building construction; but the simple sorts of construction involved in paving and steps and garden walls are seldom treated in books, and to judge by results, many architects and builders seem to be hazy about these primitive works. There is, however, one outstanding recent book, Elisabeth Beazley's *Design and Detail of the Space between Buildings* which, while it deals mainly with public spaces, is a mine of information, not easily available elsewhere, about hard landscape, with much fuller information about construction than can be given in this little book, in which moreover I want to stick as far as possible to the visual effect of the works as part of the garden design.

Not only are good books hard to come by; it is even harder to find good craftsmen who can make a good job of these simple constructions. When you find one it is a great pleasure to see how much good craftsmanship adds to the design. But if you are fussy, you may have to do it yourself.

There is a natural contrast between hard stone and soft leaf, between the necessary straightness of boundaries, paths and kerbs and the infinitely complex forms of plants. Too often gardeners seem to want to renounce this, and make everything as lax and irregular as possible. This is a pity; it is impossible anyway to escape the straight line altogether—it is bound to get you at the boundary, the road or the house—and besides, the contrast itself is piquant. Even in nature this same contrast is the theme of many of the most moving landscapes— the pines against the cliff, the woods against the shore, the reeds against the water; and it is an essential part of the magic of ruins, and of many of the great gardens of the world. It is a perfect theme for the small garden—often a rectangle, between buildings—to let the building elements be severely straight, with the falling, carpeting and thrusting forms of the plants in contrast, as if asserting the perennial renewal of nature.

Above: one of the world's great gardens—the lake shore and bridge leading to the Shokintei tea house in the Katsura Palace garden at Kyoto, built early in the 17th century
Right: one of several tiny gardens, designed to be seen while sitting at the tea ceremony in the tea houses of Ura Senke in Kyoto. A garden to be looked at rather than entered, which recreates the qualities of the natural landscape by intensely artificial means and with extremely simple materials and planting
Left: Ura Senke: the entrance path watered to welcome the visitor

Notes on the Built Elements

Fences and Walls

Fences and walls are essential for shelter and privacy and they form a big element in any garden view. On plan, they show as a thin line; but in perspective even a dwarf wall cuts off a lot of ground, and a 5 ft wall can occupy more actual space in the view, looked at as a picture, than a lawn many yards long. Walls and fences are traditionally simple and unadorned; naturally enough, for ornament applied to such utilitarian and extensive objects soon becomes boring. The exception to this rule is the decoration of individual elements—the spikes of a railing or the boards of a picket fence—where the ornament is so repetitive that it becomes part of the texture, like a fringe. Generally, the beauty of walls and fences lies in their texture and colour and their ability to resist the weather; a decaying fence spreads gloom over the whole garden.

Unlike the walls of buildings which only present one side to the weather and are warmed on the inside and protected by eaves and cornices, garden walls are totally exposed to wind, rain and frost. They call for *better* materials and workmanship than the walls of buildings, rather than the skimping they usually get. To spend as much as one can afford on permanence is often an economy in the long run; to spend 50% more may mean twice the life, or more, and rebuilding always causes havoc to neighbouring plants and climbers which may have taken years to grow.

Colour

Colour is vitally important, especially with openwork fences, such as wire mesh or railings. If you want to see through a fence, or to make it disappear into the landscape, paint it dark; if you want a visual barrier, paint it light. Black and white are always right; next in usefulness is the extremely dark olive green BS 4-051. The worst of all colours, not only on fences, but on all garden and country objects is the one most often used—a bright 'apple' green; presumably it is thought to 'go with' the green of the country and the garden, but in fact it clashes violently with every natural green, especially that of mown grass. Better to stick to black and white or neutral colours, or have a deliberate contrast with green, such as a dark red.

Wall plants

It is very pleasant to have climbing plants on walls and fences, and it is wise to make arrangements for them at the start. A few plants (see page 54) will cling to walls by themselves, and need no support; the rest need trellis or wires, at least to get started, although there are many plants which having been helped over the top of a wall will then support themselves by the tangle of their own growth. In brick and masonry walls vine eyes can be built in to new walls or hammered in (more difficult) to old walls to support a regular grid of wires, preferably plastic-covered, in black or brown. Welded steel mesh or the traditional

Two views of the 17th century
garden of the Villa Garzoni at
Collodi, an Italian Baroque
garden in the grand manner. Most
of the English designers who
copied this style merely imitated
the details—stairs, ponds and
balustrades—and failed entirely to
realise the subtle use of the site
and its levels, of which the
Italians were masters

wood trellis can be used, but should be extremely well protected with paint or preservative, as rusting and rotting is a catastrophe when the plants are established. The more unobtrusive the support, the better; for my taste, trellis is too conspicuous, and the ideal is that the plants should appear to have come naturally to cover the wall.

Masonry and Brickwork

Stone and brick stand out above all other wall materials for beauty and permanence; the older they get and the more algae and lichens they grow, the better they look.

New stone is now too expensive for most people, but one can often lay hands on old stone from road works or demolitions which is being thrown away because engineers and architects are too lazy to re-use it, and it is always worth having, especially for retaining walls. The 'dry' stone retaining wall, with joints of soil instead of mortar, is still a most effective way of making a change of level, and a perfect site for growing those plants adapted to rock crevices; it looks well even when made of a miscellaneous assortment of stones, and even slates and bricks. Bricks and stone are so intrinsically good looking that they can stand entirely without ornament, and their form cannot be too simple. Indeed, the only problem is how to provide such things as a coping to keep out wet, or piers for strength, without too much elaboration. For example, brick walls on gently sloping ground are often built with horizontal courses, their tops stepping down every few yards—an extremely fussy arrangement compared to the traditional one of letting the courses follow the slope of the ground. But horizontal courses are what they teach at schools of building, and they can be kept straight with a mason's level, whereas sloping courses need a craftsman's eye.

Bricks for garden walls must be frostproof; well burnt stock bricks (made from clay mixed with ashes, which makes them almost self-burning) are ideal. They have great frost resistance, are absorbent enough to adhere strongly to mortar, and are full of attractive colours and mottlings from the burning process, with a pleasing roughness of texture. To an inexperienced eye such bricks tend to look scruffy when held in the hand, but built into a wall their individual spots and blemishes blend, with the pattern of joints, into a rich texture; bricks which look pretty in the hand often make a dull and textureless wall.

Most books advocate damp-proof courses, even in garden walls. Though these are necessary in buildings to prevent damp rising to the interior, they perform no useful function in a free standing wall of frost proof bricks. Indeed, both at the top and the base of a wall they cut off the damp at a sharp line, which will clearly show a difference between the wet and dry bricks; moreover, the rising damp at the base, or the descending rainwater at the top, will concentrate at the damp-course joint, and this will severely try the frostproofness of the bricks.

Opposite: two views and a plan drawing of the Patio de la Ria in the Generalife at Granada. The Moorish gardens of Spain are private oases, ringing with water and shaded by trees and buildings, in utter contrast to the arid landscape outside. The form of this palace is a series of courts stepping down the hillside, fed with a small source of water which appears in rills, ponds and fountains in court after court

Photograph: Graeme Shankland

22

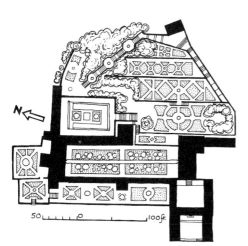

The construction of brick walls cannot be fully dealt with here, but a few main points must be made. Brick walls need a mass concrete foundation, of a size according to the bearing strength of the ground, at a depth where frost and moisture movement will not operate— 1' 6" or 2' 0" for frost, but 3' 0" or more for moisture in clay soils which shrink when dry. Mortar should be fairly weak in cement, say 1 of cement to 6 of sand; stronger mixtures are often advised, but they only increase shrinkage. Old walls in lime mortar did not shrink as walls in cement and sand do, though they were said to be more prone to damage by frost. Long walls should have expansion (really shrinkage) joints which can be worked in at piers which are often needed anyway for strength. Generally, garden walls of normal height (6 ft) should be 9 in. thick; 'half brick' 4½ in. walls are impossible to build fairface both sides because of irregularities in the bricks, are soon damaged by weather, and lack stability.

Serpentine walls with about 8 ft radius curves, 4 ft deep, though no more weatherproof, are stable at 4½ in. thick, and if you have room are pleasant and give shelter for plants or seats in their recesses. Joints are a big factor in appearance; flush joints should be cut flush with the side of the trowel and not struck or 'weathered' which gives a shiny and mechanical appearance. Joints usually look better in plain grey Portland cement; white cement, or the addition of lime, gives a much whiter joint and a much paler wall. The colour of the wall depends on brick plus joint; recessed joints, pressed back say ⅜ in., because of their shadow, affect the colour of the wall less, and make it look darker which is often an advantage. The various bonds also have an effect on appearance; especially with stock bricks when the end (or header) faces of the bricks often come out of the kiln much paler than the side (or stretcher) faces, so that English bond, with its alternate courses of headers and stretchers, can look stripey.

Blocks

There are many types of concrete block, from simple solid blocks like large bricks, to elaborate openwork blocks with various patterns of perforation, which can be built as masonry. When plain, the colour of concrete is light and can be very pleasant, though it tends to show dirt stains from weathering more obviously than brick. The appearance can be greatly varied—by different aggregates (the stone component), by brushing the surface before it has set to expose the aggregate, by embedding flints etc in the face of blocks, by ribs or other patterns, or by casting large blocks and breaking them in a shearing machine to give a 'riven' face. Colour can also be added to the cement, with rather less perceptible effect. Concrete blocks are also made in special shapes which interlock and can be built without mortar.

Slabs and sheets

Slabs of concrete, and sheets of asbestos cement and other materials can be used for fences but need posts for connection and support.

Brick bonds:

a. Flemish: alternate headers and stretchers

b. Monk: as Flemish with spaced out headers

c. English: alternate courses of headers and stretchers

d. English garden-wall, as c. but with header courses spaced out

24

1 A play garden at a children's home, by the architect Hedqvist, near Stockholm. The wall makes the garden by sheltering, enclosing and defining the space

2 A stock brick wall, coped with Portland stone, showing the tradition of sloping instead of stepping courses up a hill

3 The flint wall, with stone bonding stones and a few bricks mixed in, surrounding Meads at Winchester College. The black slots are recesses for candles, lit at festivals

4 An old brick wall at Winchester. The colour is almost entirely made of lichens and mosses

Instead of the continuous simple effect of masonry or brick walls, they present a much less simple effect of repeated bays; and the detail, capping and jointing of posts causes many aesthetic problems.

Timber

Timber of many kinds has been traditional fence material for centuries, and it is still beautiful stuff with special aptitude for small gardens and for amateur craftsmen. The main problem is rotting of the timber especially in contact with the ground or in joints and other places where damp accumulates. Rot can be forestalled and postponed by treatment with creosote and other preservatives; these usually alter the appearance of the wood and prevent the pleasing silver-grey weathering which several timbers naturally acquire.

The principle is to support the fence either on concrete or metal uprights, or on timber posts the feet of which have been carefully rot-proofed by soaking in a bath of hot creosote, or coal tar, with or without charring by fire, and keeping the rest of the fence clear of the ground altogether. The upper part can then be made of a timber which weathers well without preservative, such as oak, larch, chestnut or western red cedar, or of a cheaper timber creosoted. Timber looks and lasts extremely well when painted, especially white; but as four-coat work is essential, and needs frequent renewal, this is expensive and is usually done only on the most important fences. The detailed design of joints, cappings, etc in a timber fence, to shed water and avoid rot, can add years to its life. However, as cheapness is usually what decides one to use timber, instead of brick, one must watch that all this preserving, painting and craftsmanship doesn't add up, considering relative length of life, to more than the cost of brickwork.

Several excellent cheaper wood fences exist. Split vertical chestnut paling, bound with galvanised wire, on 4 in. posts, is excellent, and if it is tightly strained, instead of flopping about as it usually does, is a neat and tidy temporary fence. Wattle hurdles made of woven hazel, or the neater and more expensive osier, look good in informal situations. Interwoven thin sawn wood impregnated with creosote is a popular suburban fence, cheap when made of cheap wood, but not very permanent, and often spoiled by the fancy design of projecting posts; this can be avoided by cutting the posts level with the fence and having a continuous capping rail. Stockades of larch poles or railway sleepers or other chance finds can sometimes be useful.

Iron and Steel

The splendid standard cast iron fences and balustrades that filled the Victorian catalogues are, alas, no more. One can get wrought iron, as a rural industry, but it is now an expensive tailor-made job, admirable for handrails, balconies, etc. Wrought iron is durable and corrodes

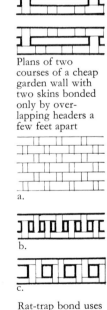

Plans of two courses of a cheap garden wall with two skins bonded only by overlapping headers a few feet apart

a.

b.

c.

Rat-trap bond uses bricks on side: a. shows pattern b. & c. alternative plans; b. stronger, but c. good for nesting boxes

A fine traditional white-painted
timber fence: only the stout posts
enter the ground; its whiteness
makes it difficult to see through

Iron railings, dark coloured,
hardly interrupt the view at all

The most invisible fence: a well
designed farm fence of steel and
wire

27

slowly, and in good hands it can achieve a simple slender elegance, contrasting beautifully with solid masonry or brickwork.

Most modern iron fences are in fact mild steel, which rusts much faster and needs very careful and frequent painting. Several good standard agricultural patterns can be got, and are useful as simple physical, but not visual, barriers.

Wire

Simple strained galvanised wire on steel posts is useful in agricultural situations, and is one of the cheapest and least obtrusive fences.

Chain link, on the other hand, though cheap, is often very ugly. It is, however, an extremely *useful* fence, rabbit proof, not very climbable, adaptable to slopes, and so on. To look neat it must be strained tight, with a level wired top; to look unobtrusive it must be *black*. The wave of the interwoven links, seen in perspective, is practically solid, and if galvanised looks almost opaque. In fact, galvanising is not too permanent in chain link, because the vibration of the loose links against one another wears it through at the crossings; better is the plastic-coated type, now available in black and olive green as well as other less suitable colours. If one is aiming at unobtrusiveness, it is of course important, with all wire fences, to remember that the *posts* can be more obtrusive than the fence; it is no use having an invisible black wire fence with staring white concrete posts.

Gates

Gates should look inviting and should be an obvious entry point: owing to their need for strength they sometimes turn out heavier and stronger looking than the fence, and this always looks a little absurd. Their tops should be the same height or lower than the rest of the barrier. It is particularly difficult to put suitable gates in chain link or other see-through fences, or on steeply sloping ground.

The Ha-Ha

The ha-ha or concealed fence, though it hardly finds a place in urban gardens, is an extremely useful device to separate even a small garden from country fields or parkland. It is of course relatively expensive, though modern earthmoving machinery makes the ditch quite cheap to dig, and the retaining wall is the expensive part. A ha-ha is equally effective, and cheaper, though it takes more room, if formed of a simple hollow with a fence in the bottom.

The ha-ha

Paving

All gardens need some hard surfaces, to stand up to foot traffic and to dry out quickly after rain. They are also useful for various garden

Simplified ha-ha with sunk fence

28

Unusual fence materials:

1 The wall of the Ryoanji at Kyoto; this is in fact a rather grand version of a traditional Japanese country fence. It is of plaster, rubbed with oil, on a stout timber frame and with a widely overhanging roof of grey glazed tiles

2 Slate and wire in Wales
3 Natural limestone slabs cleated to an iron farm fence at Kelmscott, Oxfordshire
4 The traditional "laid" thorn farm hedge
5 A fence of laid and plaited live bamboo at the Katsura Palace, Kyoto

jobs such as mixing soil and dividing plants, and essential for meals out of doors. In very small gardens it is quite sensible to pave the whole area; pockets and spaces can be left for plants and the absence of green grass can be more than made up for by lush-foliaged climbers. Such a paved garden needs less weeding—though it does need *some*, paving joints being an attractive bed for seeds. Provided there is good, well-drained topsoil below, *and the paving is open-jointed*, it actually seems to help the growth of plants, probably by conserving moisture. Pavings which are continuous and impervious, like in situ concrete, asphalt or tarmacadam, cut off air and water from the soil and are inimical to plant life.

The first thing to remember about paving is that *the soil carries the weight*, both of the paving and its traffic. The paving is there to spread the load of the traffic on the soil, and to give a surface which does not puddle, or disintegrate. Some sinking of the surface after laying does not matter, but it must be an even sinking, not hollows here and there. For ordinary pedestrian traffic, paving is normally laid (unless the subsoil is gravel or chalk which doesn't need strengthening) over a base of hardcore (broken bricks or stones) ashes or coarse gravel not less than 3 in. thick, well consolidated by ramming and rolling. This is 'blinded' by ashes, and the paving surface—gravel, slabs, bricks, etc laid over it. Gravel goes direct on to the blinding; slabs and bricks on to a 2 in. bed of sand. It is quite useless to put a thin layer of concrete over the ground in the hope of strengthening the paving; if the ground is going to sink, this will not stop it—indeed, it will tend to crack at widely separated points, so that instead of a slight overall unnoticeable sinkage, you get very noticeable stepped cracks here and there.

Left and opposite: paving begins as a simple reinforcement of the ground surface

The surface between the limestone walkways is of flints, etc., laid in a very weak mix of lime and sand (Winchester College)

30

Granite setts in grass
at Viborg in Denmark

Brick in soil and sand, with grass and weeds.
I like this, but not everyone does!

Gravel

Gravel is one of the cheapest pavings and has many virtues: it is porous and lets air and water through to roots; it has a pleasing informal look; when the texture is right it gives a smooth firm surface which can be swept. Good path gravel is composed of coarse sand and clay, sometimes with a little chalk; the proportions of sand and clay must be exactly right—enough sand to ensure drainage, and no mud, in wet weather and enough clay to ensure binding, and no dust, in dry. Many gravels fail in this, and the best path gravels are expensive; but the coarser clayey 'hoggin' can be used for the base, with the path gravel for the top 2 in. Two disadvantages: frost heaves it up and calls for re-rolling, and it grows weeds.

Tarmacadam

Tarmac is small stones, bound with coal tar or bitumen. It is an impervious paving, especially when new, and can kill established trees if put over large areas of their root systems. It is laid over a base, like gravel, and needs to be rolled against a firm edge. Limestone chippings make the best tarmac, as they absorb the binder, and they also weather to a pleasing, light silvery grey. It is sometimes made with a gravel aggregate and a reduced bitumen content, which gives a slightly less durable surface but one very pleasant to look at—the black soon wears off the gravel leaving it looking very like an ordinary gravel path. Tarmac does not allow weeds to set seed, but weeds buried underneath it will come straight through it; before laying either tarmac or gravel, it is wise to treat the site with weed killer.

Unit Pavings
Construction

The principle of laying pavings made of small units is the same for stone and concrete slabs, bricks, setts and cobbles. A base of hardcore or gravel, blinded with ashes, is followed by a bed of sand or sand-soil mixture. The units are firmly bedded into the sandy layer. Slabs require the sand to be hammered firm under the edge of each one by tamping blows with a small heavy hammer at 45 degrees. Joints can be fairly tight, or wider, up to say ½ in., with sand and soil brushed in. Bricks and setts are settled into the sand bed, with joints ⅜ in. to ½ in. wide down which stone chippings are brushed. The chippings must be big enough to jam tight in the joints and hold the units firm; any units loosened by a tread will immediately be jammed tight again by the chippings; fine sand and soil can then be brushed into the joints, and this must be done again and again till the joints are filled. Rounded cobbles—the best are the thin fish-shaped ones, used with their backs upwards—are hammered in to a rather fine sand-soil mixture; the rounded bases cause this to jam up tight between each cobble; more

1 Traditional path of York stone, margined with cobbles; architect: Lord Holford (King's College, Cambridge)

2 The Miyuki path of the Katsura Palace garden: a mosaic of small dark stones from the Kano River, bedded neatly together in sand and mud

3 A path in the author's garden of York stone which tapers by about 9 in. This gives an illusion of distance, and makes it easier to use stones of assorted sizes. The path is bordered by a 4 in gravel channel, and a kerb raised 4 in to the bed

is brushed into the surface.

It is *not* necessary to point any of these pavings with mortar; it disfigures and stains the paving and the frost will pick it out in small bits leaving a scruffy gap-toothed effect. Round cobbles are sometimes wrongly laid in a cement mortar bed: the bed shrinks, water gets under the cobbles, and frost lifts them out; whereas in sand and soil, if they move at all it is only to settle ever more firmly into the bed. Some ancient pavings, especially when made of an assortment of flints, cobbles, and stones of various shapes, were bedded into extremely weak mortar made of one part lime to about 15 parts sand; this seems slightly firmer than plain sand and soil, but it is essentially weak enough to allow the units, if loosened by frost, to bed down again; and there are many very ancient pavings in sand and soil only which have stood for centuries.

Brick

Bricks for paving must be frost proof; well- or over-burnt stocks are ideal. Harder still, but tending to slipperiness, are blue engineering bricks. Bricks can be laid on their 3 in. edge or on their $4\frac{1}{2}$ in. side; the former exposes the good face which the brickmaker intended to be seen, and gives a firmer paving because of the extra depth; the latter exposes the bed face which is sometimes of poor texture, but it uses one-third less bricks and is quite good enough for ordinary use, especially with stocks which have a pleasing texture on their bed faces.

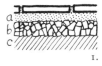

1.

Setts

Granite setts are expensive when new but can sometimes be had from demolitions of old roads, and these, having one face worn smooth, are particularly good for gardens. They range in size from $4'' \times 4''$ cubes to $6'' \times 5'' \times 10''$; the smaller ones are easier to handle and more in scale with small gardens.

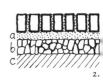

2.

Cobbles

The smooth fish-shaped cobbles, of small size, are now rare, compared with the large round tennis ball kind. The thin ones are prettier, and when laid very tight, each one touching the next, make one of the neatest of all pavings. Both cobbles and setts are fairly daunting to walk on, and are often used as margins to slab-paved paths to discourage straying on to grass. They are, of course, damaging to mower blades, and wherever grass marches with cobbles there must be a narrow margin of flat stone, flush with the grass, to mow against.

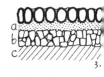

3.

Unit pavings:
1. Stone or concrete slabs
2. Bricks or setts
3. Cobbles
a. Sand or ashes mixed with soil
b. Hardcore (rammed broken brick or stone)
c. Subsoil
(scale 1/24)

Stone slabs

For beauty and permanence, stone is unrivalled. It is indeed sad to see how in towns all over Britain fine old stone pavings are being replaced by concrete slabs; doubly so, as the economy of the operation is false—stone paving costs about three times as much as concrete and lasts at least ten times as long. But concrete is 'easy to lay'—easy that is to lay badly by merely dealing out the slabs, like playing cards, on a bed of sand, and pointing with mortar, a job which lasts a decade at best.

A garden entirely paved in red
brick, by Lawrence Halprin,
San Francisco

Garden, stairs, walls and paving,
all of the beautiful pink-white
limestone of Jerusalem.
Architect: H. Rau

The old York stones, being of various thicknesses, *must* be bedded separately, as any slabs should be if they are going to stay put.

York stone is a perfect paving, dense and uniform in texture, easy to cut clean and straight, frost proof, with pleasing slight variations in colour. But most other stones can be used, especially in gardens, where durability can take second place to texture and colour. New stone is now too expensive for most people, but anyone making a garden should keep an eye open for the old and often beautifully weathered stones which often lie unwanted in demolished or derelict buildings. Sometimes one can find large stones—steps, copings or kerbs—which in a small garden can become seats or other objects of almost sculptural value.

Concrete

Concrete slabs are often a necessary substitute for stone, inferior though they are in colour and texture. Nor do they weather so well, tending instead to wear out, with cracks and frost-nibbled corners. However, they vary a good deal. The granite aggregate slabs are more durable, but much more difficult for amateurs to cut—not that any concrete slabs can be cut like York stone. Others can be got with various aggregates and improved textures; but it is better to accept the fact that one is working with concrete and avoid the more elaborately coloured and 'olde worlde' textured slabs which lack the strength of good concrete in all senses of the word and are yet only travesties of stone.

Concrete can also be used in situ. It should be laid not less than 4 in. thick on a base of hardcore, in bays not more than 10 ft square, with expansion joints between them. The surface texture can be infinitely varied by exposing the aggregate, by brushing with water before it is set, or by embedding crushed stones in the surface. Smooth rounded pebbles such as pea gravel should be avoided in such surfaces as they are suprisingly slippery. The surface can also be ribbed by tamping with boards, dimpled or pricked with studded rollers, and so on; but make experiments first—the final hardening is irrevocable!

Polygonal paving

Irregularly shaped stones can be fitted into beautiful patterns. Not, one hastens to add, in the manner which has the apt title of 'crazy paving', any old broken stones jumbled together; but a carefully fitted interlocked pattern of stones in which the joints of constant width make an elaborate network—*opus incertum*, as the Romans called it. There are some wonderful examples of how varied such work can be in the old Japanese gardens.

Drainage

In a garden it should not be necessary to drain surface water into gullies; but it is wise to give paths and especially terraces a slight fall

Paving as art. The famous path in the Katsura Palace garden at Kyoto, in which stones large and small, regular and irregular in shape, and of varying colours, are related to one another with a sculptor's care to avoid even temporary puddles after rain; and if the terrace is wide, it is as well not to tip the surplus water straight into a flowerbed, but to have a gutter of sand or shingle and a kerb to the bed.

Sweeping

The paving patterns of a garden are lost under leaves and rubbish unless frequently swept clean. One should think of this while designing: there are many small details—the gutter just mentioned, the raised kerb to a bed—which all add up to a much lighter job of cleaning up. If you have beautiful stone paving it is worth scrubbing it occasionally with water, especially in town atmospheres, to reveal the colour which dust will have obscured. It is wonderful how a garden is transformed by this sweeping and scrubbing: not unnaturally, it is an essential part of the upkeep of Japanese gardens, which depend so much on paving, and an important visitor will always find the garden swept and newly sprinkled with water. There is an ancient story from Japan of an old man who had his son to sweep his garden, but he was not satisfied, and the son went over it all again. 'Still not perfect,' said the old man, and he went down the path and shook a tree which dropped a leaf or two on to the shining stones. Now the visitors could come in!

Weeding

All paving will need some weeding. It is possible with small units—bricks and setts—to allow grass to take over and actually to mow it with a blade set high—a sort of reinforced lawn. But generally the paving patterns should be seen. The ideal is perhaps to have every joint filled with moss, with all grass and weeds hand picked out. Most people will settle for some compromise, and many will use the new granular weed killers which lie in the joints and can even be used, at exactly the right strength, to kill grass and weeds while allowing moss to grow. Large plants which seed themselves in paving—such as Foxgloves and Mulleins—are, however, very welcome and tend to grow finely.

Steps

Steps can be one of the most beautiful features of a garden. They are one of the elements which give 'scale' as architects call it. Every human being has a sense built-in to his feet, as it were, of the natural size of a step; other elements share this quality—the hand-height balustrade, the head-clearing door, and so on. By reducing or exaggerating the size of such elements, the apparent size of everything in sight can be changed. Indeed, in using deliberately huge elements—such as the 'heroic' scale of St Peter's in Rome—the architect can persuade the spectator that he is *himself* of heroic size (something similar happens with American motor cars!). In a small garden, on the other hand, the problem is

Two Japanese landscapes in Kyoto in which steps are used, not only to change level, but as part of the architectural composition, to define space and link buildings together: the broad approach to the temple Nansenji; and inside the precinct of the temple Daitokuji usually to make the space look larger.

Almost all garden steps are too steep. One's pace and gait out of doors is quite different from indoors and the 12″×6″ stair that looks generous and easy indoors gives a breakneck precipitous effect in the open. A 5 in. riser with 15 in. tread is the standard landscape step, but one can go much shallower than this, at least up to 20″×4″. You should be able to *run* up them, as Gertrude Jekyll says. There should always be a slight outward fall on each step, say ¼in., to throw water off.

Steps can be shallower still in a stepped ramp—a very gentle slope, say 1 in 15, with steps at wide intervals for several paces to each step. Each step must give an *odd* number of paces to avoid coming down on the same foot each time, and the pace can be taken as about 2′ 6″; thus 7′ 6″ treads are all right while 5′ 0″ or 10′ 0″ are wrong.

Alternatively there are a few situations where extremely steep steps can be right, as long as one wants a forbidding effect rather than an inviting one.

Steps are an integral part of the paved surface, and should look like a natural extension of it, but they can naturally be more solid, with larger slabs and heavy edges to withstand wear. Wide steps can have solid treads with the back of each step filled in with smaller stones or even gravel and plants. The foundation of steps should always be a bit more substantial than that of the paving, and the main risers should be set in concrete to prevent them from moving; a flight of steps is a kind of retaining wall and there is always a tendency for it to slide. The width of flights is important: for a generous and easeful effect, the wider the better; and some steps can continue on to become walls or kerbs or others lines in the garden. Occasionally extremely informal and irregular steps are good, but they must obey the rules of pace and tread. A good informal stair can be made of logs or baulks of well-preserved timber, with turfed treads; but the cutting of the grass is a fiddling job.

The arrangement of the sides of steps in banks is always difficult—whether to leave the steps to run against the bank, and if so, above the bank or recessed into it, or against a wall or coping. Informal sides can be pleasant, but can involve awkward trimming of grass.

Steps tend to collect windblown leaves and rubbish, especially in the angles against side walls. A very pleasing arrangement, originally I think Chinese, which makes sweeping easier and also gives a clean and airy effect to the flight, is to stop each tread back about 4½ in. from the side wall, and have a sloping gutter against the wall, passing the steps at the level of the bottom of each riser. This little sunken Chinese channel is also useful at any margin between paving and kerb or wall. Stepping stones are useful to prevent wear in grass lawns; again, for easy walking they must be at 2′ 6″ centres. They tend to sink slightly in grass, even when firmly laid, as the grass tends to build itself up with growth and top dressing, and it helps to have them ¼ in. high to

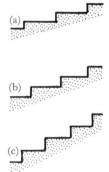

Gradients for garden steps
(a) 4″×16″ desirable
(b) 5″×15″ standard
(c) 6″×12″ too steep for outdoors

1 York stone steps, beautifully designed
for a slow, hesitating approach to the
Kennedy Memorial at Runnymede.
By Geoffrey Jellicoe. The junction of
the steps to the sloping granite sett
paving is ingeniously done
2 Steps of wood, with a flat iron bar as
tread, and handrails of peeled logs,
at the Borgvold Park, Viborg, Denmark
3 A sloping 'Chinese Channel' to
separate steps from a flanking wall,
which prevents rubbish collecting in
the angles and makes sweeping easier
4 Steps carried out to form structural
lines of the garden; designed by
Margaret Maxwell

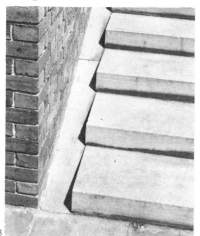

begin with. The mower can run over them, but the grass will grow over at the sides; if you don't like it, you can trim with a razor blade knife thrust vertically down round the stones.

Water

Nothing is more delightful in a garden than water: it is a symbol of life and renewal; it suggests coolness and luxury, and it brings with it movement, reflections, pleasant sounds; it attracts birds and animals, and it can itself be a home for plants, fish and a whole fauna of its own. But no garden element is less understood, and failures with water are common.

Balanced-Life Ponds

First, one must decide whether one wants sparkling clear water in clean, painted or tiled basins, with no plants, no pond life, no mud; or natural organic water in a 'balanced-life' condition *with* plants, pond life and mud.

The former is practically unattainable; water attracts dirt—the dust and leaves which blow across terraces or lawns are caught by a pond, and sink to the bottom; and all water in daylight grows algae. So that water basins to appear absolutely clean must be scrubbed out very frequently—several times a week, in towns—and the water itself must be chemically sterilised to prevent algae and insect life starting up. The only examples of 'clean' water usually seen are in closed-circuit city fountains, or in swimming pools.

Balanced-life water, on the other hand, is easy and manages itself. It must have soil, in which plants grow to provide oxygen for fishes and other pond life which provide carbon dioxide for the plants; insects and snails scavenge the decaying organic matter, fish keep down an excess of insects, and the whole system can support itself for very long periods. A small stagnant pond, with less than two cubic yards of water constructed by my father and myself in 1928, was in quite good order in 1965, with healthy descendants of the original fish and plants; the water had never been changed, and it had been absolutely untouched since my father's death in 1952. In fact, a pond, newly filled with water, even without planting, will start with algae, attract water insects, and gather mud; and after a rather unsavoury early period will end up as a balanced-life pond complete with plants, brought by birds, and eventually even fish. But this is a long process, and one can install it, plants, fish, insects and all, quite easily in a few months.

A balanced life pond needs a waterproof base and sides, of puddled clay, plastic sheet, concrete 4 in. or 6 in. thick, or brickwork rendered in cement and sand. It should be not less than 1' 6" deep nor more than 3' 0", to let sunlight in and start growth early in spring, and to be the right depth for waterlilies. It can have overflow bays for bog gardens

1 Water seen against the sun in the
Patio de la Ria in the Generalife at
Granada. The Spanish gardens have
a smaller *quantity* of water than the
Italian, but it is led everywhere and
made to perform again and again at
each descending level. Photograph:
Spanish National Tourist Office

2 A stream in the garden of the
Imperial Palace, Kyoto; clear in the
shallow over stones, dark and
gloomy in the pit (which is
constructed like a wooden tub)

3 The Japanese ponds are made
muddier by the great carp, which
appear gold and mysterious as they
touch the surface

and can form part of a little stream system, with a pump to recirculate the water. It is good to have a small drip fountain or other method of topping up the water and sinking the surface dust in dry weather. It should have 6 in. of plain loam on the bottom to grow oxygenating plants; waterlilies and other special plants which are greedy for manure can be grown in baskets or compartments of the same soil mixed with cow manure or bonemeal. At the outset, some microscopic pond life, especially Daphnia, with some mud and weeds, should be introduced from an old pond. Later, when these and the plants have had time to become established, small fish, frogs, newts, etc, can be introduced. The prettiest fish, in my view, are the small natives such as roach and rudd and above all the busy stickleback, always courting and fighting and building visible nests if you give him little sunny ledges. Carp, on the other hand, including goldfish, are comparatively dull and ponderous creatures, and spend a lot of time disturbing the bottom and muddying the water. Such small ponds can be frozen all but solid without harming the fish.

Designing Water

The beauty of water is subtle and complex; it lies not so much in the stuff itself—a colourless liquid, after all—as in the phenomena occurring in certain special situations: reflection, for example, depends on the lighting of the reflected scene, the stillness of the surface film, the dark colour of the bottom of the pond, the angle of vision of the spectator, and so on; and designing with water is largely a matter of understanding these optical effects, and arranging for them to occur. Water has also extremely intractable qualities such as remaining level when at rest, or flowing downhill. In a natural landscape, water always lies in a natural inevitable position; in a garden, one can easily put water in an unnatural position. On a gentle slope, for example, one can arrange a pond where no natural pond would occur, and because the eye accepts the unnoticeable slope as level, the water will appear to be tilted! This can easily happen in small gardens, which are very seldom quite level. On the other hand, this quality of flowing downhill and finding its own level means that one source of water, given a sloping site, can be made to perform over and over again. It is possible, as the Spanish gardens show, to make a whole series of palace courts ring with water from one very tiny source—beside such art the great Italian cascades look like conspicuous waste!

Water as a reflecting medium:

Above: in the Wolf Pool, Brecon, can be seen all the conditions of reflection; on the right, in the shade of trees, no reflection and a clear view into the depths; on the left, first half-reflected banks, and then bright sky reflections and dazzle of sunlight

A dark onyx coloured pool in the New Jersey Pine Barrens: black peaty water, black muddy bottom, and still surface protected from the wind

Perfect reflecting conditions: sunlit buildings in shady water; Amsterdam

Reflection

Reflection is probably the most sought-after quality of water in gardens. First, there must be something to reflect; and it must be sunlit, and either near the pond edge or, if farther back, above it. The surface of the water must be still and clean and the bottom dark coloured. Most brilliant reflection comes when the water is in the shade and one looks across it to a sunlit object; but water usually looks best, and grows plants best, in the sun; water cools the heat of a sunlit space, but increases the damp and gloom of shade, which though a virtue in Arabia is a fault in England.

Noise and Fountains

The noise of falling water is grateful in the heat of the sun, depressing in shade. Fountains, which depend also on the sparkle of reflected light, should always be sunlit. Fountains disturb the surface and break up reflections; they also sink dust and when they stop the surface is clean and its reflections more brilliant than ever. Sometimes one can arrange to have noise *and* reflection, as in the Court of the Myrtles in the Alhambra in Granada.

Large fountains need room to be blown by the wind, and have no place in small gardens. Yet the noise of falling water is desirable. It is not enough simply to scale down a large fountain to say 3 ft in height; it will simply make a depressing piddling noise. It is better to have a drip fountain. Water dripping from one bowl into another makes a musical note, and if several bowls or ledges are arranged one over the other, a considerable volume of noise can be got from an extremely small supply of water. The bowls should be stone or concrete, about an inch deep, exactly level, with an undercut drip all round, and a trickle of water laid on to the top one.

Margins

When water fills its container to the brim it brings feelings of luxury and plenty; if it sinks, of deficiency and drought. Moreover, water reflects its own margin; so that if it is 6 in. down, the reflection doubles it and it seems to have sunk a foot. Any exposed margin above the waterline is liable to be stained and water-marked, which adds to the sad effect.

A very pleasing thing near margins is to have some large flat stones near the edge, an inch or two below the surface of the water; the visibility of these stones in the water, combined with the darkness of the bottom of the pond, gives an impression of clearness and great depth of water. Such ledges make excellent bird baths and, a little deeper, nesting places for sticklebacks.

A pool can look very pretty margined with grass, but is not easy to keep. Ponds attract people, and edges get worn. It is good to pave

The fountain in the Court of the Myrtles in the Alhambra at Granada: the fountain splashes noisily in its little basin, but the water is led along a narrow channel, which stills it, to enter the pool gently and without disturbing the reflections on its surface

Photograph: Gordon Michell

A fountain by Walter Rossow in the German Pavilion at the Brussels Exhibition of 1958. The water issues from the centre of the convex slabs, and fans out over the polished stone. The whole effect depends on the fountain being in the shade of the tree, and the reflections of light coming from the sky beyond

Sloping water: an optical illusion created by the dominant sloping lines of the balustrades; the Medici Fountain in the Luxembourg garden, Paris

margins, and for the paving to slope imperceptibly away from the edge, to avoid rain showers washing mud into the water.

The Plants

England shares with the north west Pacific coast of America the best climate in the world for the growing of plants; it will not grow tropical plants, of course, which can't stand frost, but with some modifications —a sheltering wall, a raised bed, some woodland shade—it will grow almost everything else. This is bad for gardens: in England they too easily become crowded Noah's Arks, one of everything; or hospitals where intensive care is lavished on wretched moribund plants which it is the owner's pride to keep alive. The funny thing about this is that these very plants all have somewhere in the world where they grow like—and indeed *are*—weeds; if you go there you are likely to find the native garden maniacs struggling to grow *our* weeds. This is a matter of personal taste; mine is for plants in the pink of condition, looking as if they thought it was the garden of Eden. This doesn't mean native plants only—some are wonderful, others brought into the care and shelter of the garden clearly don't know how to behave, and get out of hand—but it does mean growing plants which like your place. There is no lack of plants; whether your garden is all sun or shade, sand or clay, peat or chalk, there are still vast numbers of beautiful plants to choose from which can wax fat with you.

Indeed, the choice is frightening. No one can know all the tens of thousands of species in the Royal Horticultural Society's *Dictionary of Gardening*. But to make a garden, you must know at least a few plants well—not only their names, but their habits and appearance at all times of year, their likes and dislikes, their propagation, and so on. Again, it is a question of observation and love, helped by visits to gardens where things are labelled, the keeping of a card index of notes on your favourite plants, the reading of books and listening to those who know. You may, of course, be mad about plants and know thousands; but you can make a perfect garden with a few; the essence is to know the ones you do know really well. The great Japanese gardens have an astonishingly small plant list, but every plant is a tried and trusted component in a tradition of gardening.

Latin Names

It is impossible to get to know many plants without using the binomial system devised by Linnaeus in 1753 to help us all. A lot of sentimental nonsense is talked about English names; true, some are beautiful, but for every Elecampane or Samphire there are a hundred which are simply gauche translations of the Latin name, like Fig-leaved Goosefoot. Nor are the English names specific enough to enable you to track down the species in a book, which is the first essential to learning about

The elegance of Cannabis sativa made it a favourite Victorian summer bedding plant especially in town gardens (scale 1/15)

48

1 Solomon's seal (Polygonatum),
  a plant of beautiful form,
  which needs to stand alone so
  that the curve of its stems can
  be seen
2 and 3 show stages of growth:
  see how the stems come up
  fast and straight at first, and
  then bend sharply into their
  beautiful slow curve
4 Yucca gloriosa—which has
  beauty of form and colour in
  leaf and flower; a fine contrast
  between the strong shapes of
  the leaves and the delicate
  haphazard poise of the flowers

it. The system of Latin names makes reference easier by dividing the process into two stages—first the genus, by the generic name, and second the species, by the specific name—but English names ignore generic relationships. (Elecampane belongs to the genus Inula; but its close relative *Inula conyza* is called Ploughman's Spikenard; Spikenard in the Bible is an Indian herb, of the genus *Nardostachys,* which belongs to another family altogether. Another of the same genus, *Inula crithmoides,* is called Golden Samphire; in fact, its Latin name means 'the Samphire-like Inula' and Samphire itself is *Crithmum maritimum* of the Umbelliferous family.)

Plant Character

Every species of plant, like every other living thing, has its own recognisable form, in which its beauty lies. This form is related to the way the plant grows in its natural habitat. Almost all plants look beautiful somewhere, but to be useful in a garden, a plant must have the sort of form which looks well on its own, and doesn't need, for example, to lean for support on grasses, or hide its lack of lower leaves among the herbage of lower plants. It should also have some permanence—or at least, like the best annuals, make up for its transience by some special display.

Consider always how plants grow together in the wild, forming natural associations in which there is always a balance between survival and extinction. How different are the patterns of woodland, heath and seashore; in each the forces at work—the shade and the shelter of the trees, the wind and wet of the heath, the salt and sun and drought of the seashore—dominate the environment and determine the form and method of growth of the component plants. The beauty of these natural groupings of plants, as part of an ecological system, is the source of the beauty of gardens. Not that one can ever copy such scenes, or would want to; but in the understanding of how they happen lies the ability to plant a garden.

Gardens are extremely artificial environments—they may be tiny paved and walled spaces with a mere handful of plants—but even in these, the plants can and should look as though planted by nature herself.

In certain situations, I would claim that even an artificially trained or clipped plant—even a *hedge*—can have this look of divine harmony.

Flowers

Most gardeners think too much about flowers, and not enough about the form and grace of the whole plant. So you *hate* flowers, people say: absolutely not! I think them far too beautiful to be used as mere colouring matter, or as a kind of quantitative proof of gardening skill, or as a smack in the eye for the chap next door.

The charm of flowers is best seen at close quarters; with a contrasting

Gillenia trifoliata. The sinuous red stems and lopsided flowers give this American plant a butterfly grace (scale ⅓)

1

2

1 An association of Canadian dogwood
(Cornus canadensis) with Sphagnum, ferns,
lilies, etc, in the wild garden at Wisley.
The gardener has kept a delicate balance
by occasional interference only
2 Mossy Saxifrages, Saxifraga cuneifolia,
Anemone pulsatilla, etc, in a garden the
author as a boy made with his father. Such
arrangements are very permanent: this one
was planned before 1930 and photographed,
after much neglect, in 1954
3 Plants growing together in the wild:
such plants as the harebell (Campanula
rotundifolia) need support from grasses and
other plants. It is intensely difficult in the
garden to achieve the harmony of these
natural associations

3

background; in a revealing light, perhaps from behind to illuminate their texture. Often they look best a little isolated from one another, or a clump of flowers thinning out at the edges into other kinds of flowers, or into greenery. Again, consider nature, where flowers seldom present themselves in huge heaps of solid colour, but in drifts above the meadow grass, or tall in the shade of trees, or stuck like jewels to the face of rocks.

Again, flowers are far too beautiful to be 'improved' by the methods now made available by science to the horticultural trade. Every year, in the flower shows and journals, new faces appear on old familiar stems: bigger petals, more petals, brighter petals, double flowers, striped flowers, bunched tight flowers; all new, but few more beautiful than before. Of course, flower breeders have always wanted the best strains. Even in nature plants vary, and over the centuries wonderful things have been done with many hundreds of species; one has only to think of the Rose, the Carnation and the Lily. But now new and fiercer weapons of change are to hand. Improved understanding of the chromosome structure of plants, and new techniques such as radiation allied to a market pressure from a public which can easily be persuaded that new means better, is giving the plant breeders ideas which used only to be found in the motor industry—a new model every year, and built-in obsolescence. This would matter less if it did not mean that many of the new plants, which are not only ugly but often also of poor constitution, tend to replace older and more desirable plants in nurserymen's catalogues; fortunately, there are still nurserymen who know what good plants are, and specialise in supplying them.

Placing Plants

It is too easily assumed that a garden consists of beds for plants, paths and a lawn. In fact, plants can be grown in many different situations, and the ordinary bed is by no means the best for all plants. Many look well in isolation, or hanging from walls, or thrusting through the joints of paving or steps, or in pots and containers.

Beds

The main advantage of beds is that they can be cultivated, manured and renewed more easily than isolated pockets. The traditional herbaceous border, magnificent though it is, takes a deal of labour to keep going, and has a limited if glorious season. It is better to include a backbone at least of very permanent plants, such as shrubs or very long-lived perennials, specially chosen for winter elegance, with bays amongst them where more ephemeral plants can come and go. In order to display the form of the plants well, vary the heights and isolate tall plants amongst low ones; allow Lilies to push up through low shrubs or ground cover; and break the edge of the border with jutting

Plants of extremely strong form often look well in large pots

Plants which bear flowers in spikes are often very beautiful and striking in gardens:

1 and 2. The beauty of spikes depends on their form. The grace of the wild foxglove lies in its gently bending and tapering spire, the flowers all on one side and the stem bending that way. How can it be thought that the deformed foxglove at the Chelsea Show is "improved"— with its flowers standing stiffly out all round its ramrod stem, and all the charm of its gentle ancestor gone?

3 The white Eremurus at Sissinghurst, looking very fine against its dark background of yew

4 Cimicifuga racemosa, a lovely American plant, whose spikes all lean gracefully towards the light; again best seen against a dark background

promontories on which some plants can be seen standing out on their own.

Narrow beds or pockets at the foot of walls are very good sites for plants with good foliage, such as Irises or Solomon's Seal. If south facing, they can be very dry, especially if they carry the roots of climbers as well; but a number of plants such as nerines love these baked situations.

Always have some stones or slabs between a bed and a lawn; it saves damage to the grass when working the border, and allows cushiony plants to fall over the margin, without getting tangled with the grass. It also helps to raise all beds slightly, with at least a 4 in. kerb: it gives definition to the edge and helps drainage; and again, plants droop over it gracefully. In heavy soils on wet land, it pays to raise beds quite high, say 1′ 6″ above the paths, for drainage, with dry stone or brick walls.

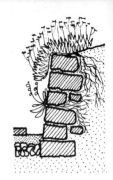

A dry stone wall as edge to terrace or raised bed: section (scale 1/48)

Beds are often put against walls as a matter of course; but if you have enough space, they are even better isolated, and seen from all round, leaving the walls for climbers.

Dry walls

Dry walls, of stones or blocks with soil joints, built with a slight batter, are excellent sites for plants whose habitat is a rock face and which grow most gracefully in a horizontal position. Some form rosettes, like the silver Saxifrages and Lewisias; some have tufts of leaves and ascending flowers, like Wall Pennywort; some make a cascading mat, like Dianthus. Many cliff plants are adapted to shade, like Wall Pennywort and most of the ferns.

Paving

If there is a good depth of fertile soil under slab paving, it makes a good site for plants. The slabs conserve moisture and retain warmth. Small gaps can be left for the larger plants, but it is surprising how small a crevice will suffice for big self-seeded plants like Foxgloves and Hollyhocks. It is possible to fill all the joints with a tiny turf of mat-forming plants, which will stand treading and even, like the Thymes, reward it with scent.

Tufted plants with their sword-like leaves, such as Iris sibirica and Liriope, look particularly well in paving, where their fine grasslike form can be seen, instead of being hidden amongst other plants.

Rocks

The rock garden, according to the precepts of Jekyll and Farrer, is now severely out of fashion. But it was a setting for a particularly beautiful sort of plant which, as small permanent pretty and largely evergreen perennials, are exactly what the small garden needs. The rock garden was in essence a raised bed, with good drainage and plenty of crevice and rock face sites for rosette, tuft or mat-forming plants. Except for weeding, it is a trouble-free form of gardening. The

Umbilicus rupestris: a plant of damp cliffs and walls

54

1 Maidenhair Spleenwort (asplenium) shows beautiful adaptation to its rockface or wall habitat. See how the lower fronds stand out from the wall to get the light while the upper ones, flattened against the wall, turn their leaflets horizontal to the light like the slats of a Venetian blind

2 Lewisia Tweedyi, another rock plant at home in a wall

3 Liriope, a plant of modest flower but wonderfully graceful evergreen leaves

4 A kerb and flat stones at the edge of a border allows plants to fall over the edge without spoiling the lawn

old rockeries felt bound to imitate crags and valleys and natural strata, all of which looked incongruous in the average plot. But it is possible to build a stone garden for such plants, in a very small compass, and there is no reason why it should try to echo the alps.

Climbing plants

There are only a few plants which will adhere to walls by themselves. They are invaluable. By far the best—perhaps the most beautiful plant in the landscape architect's repertoire—is the common ivy, Hedera helix. It has lots of varieties with larger or smaller or sharper or variegated leaves, but none improves on the lustrous green of the original type. Contrary to common belief, it does no harm to—indeed *preserves*—sound masonry or brickwork; but its habit of inserting shoots into cracks means it will eventually penetrate and destroy ruins, and of course it is disastrous to slates and tiles. An old plant can be 'pulled'—the old leaves and twigs break off neatly in the hand—and the mat of branches on the wall will at once cover itself with new and brilliant leaves. It will grow on buildings, walls, trees, stumps; it can be trained on wires or pergolas into any shape; it is the best of all ground covers—a paragon among plants.

The other self-clingers are several species of vine known as Virginia Creeper or Boston Ivy—the self-clinging ones are Vitis inconstans and Vitis quinquefolia; beautiful, with fierce autumn colour, but deciduous; and three evergreen plants, Hydrangea petiolaris, Schizophragma hydrangeoides and Pileostegea viburnioides. The first beautiful and common, the others similar but rare.

Most other climbers need help of wires or pergola. Walls protect them, especially if facing south west, from cold, but pergolas show them off best, and, if Britain were not a bit too shady already, would be essential features of every garden. Pergolas should be very simply and stoutly built to last as long as their plants; they should be *not less than* 8' 6" high, because plants hang down and grab at your head, and plenty wide enough, for similar reasons.

Hedges

Hedges pose a dilemma—quick growing and always needing cutting like privet, or slow growing and cut only once or twice a year like yew. The quick growing ones are also greedy and dry out the ground in nearby beds unless their roots are kept out by vertical sheeting underground. The really disastrous ones are quick growers which are not quite hardy, like Lonicera nitida and Cupressus macrocarpa, which raise great hopes and then die in patches in the first bad winter. The three classic hedges are Yew, Holly and Beech, all slow, and all perfect except for one fault each: Yew poisons cattle, Holly catches fire easily if someone throws a cigarette into its fallen leaves, Beech is not evergreen. But beech holds its dry red leaves all winter. Hornbeam is a

A silver Saxifrage: typical alpine crevice plant (scale ¼)

56

1 The herb garden at Sissinghurst; a
most subtle grouping of plants
depending entirely on texture and
colour of leaves and plant form, and
their contrast with stone

2 Dielytra spectabilis, beautifully
placed at Sissinghurst in a lead·tank,
so that the beauty of its drooping
leaves and hanging flowers—often
lost amongst other plants in a border
—is clearly seen

close runner up, a sort of poor man's beech.

One can, of course, go right away from the classical hedges and have a living fence of almost any shrub of the right habit. The most impenetrable of all fences is probably one of the hardy Bamboos grown solid and thick.

Water Plants

Water plants need sun. A pond needs underwater plants to oxygenate the water. Floating leaved plants enhance water wonderfully and their leaves are more important than flowers. Waterlilies give you both; Nymphaea alba and some of its less garish varieties are the most beautiful and reliable; the wild Yellow Waterlily, Nuphar luteum, is splendid but a ferociously rampant grower. Many other pond plants have floating leaves; some like Limnanthemum, are tiny and good for small pools.

The Reeds, Irises and Rushes which stand in water should be placed so that their reflections can be seen. As they have similar strong shapes, not quite identical, each kind looks best in isolation rather than jumbled with others.

One can always arrange boggy ground near a pool and many families of plants have bog-loving members. A bog looks soggy and disgusting unless fairly covered with plants; there are a number of delicate little plants which will wander about and cover the blackness. Some of the grandest herbaceous plants like wet—several Rhubarbs (*Rheum*), Rodgersia, and the great Chilian Gunnera manicata, with spiny rhubarb leaves 6 ft across.

Lawns

Lawns are too big a subject. But don't get discouraged by specialist books or lawn enthusiasts, for whom a weedless grass lawn is a sacred ideal. Some of the nicest lawns have hardly any grass, and I actually prefer the texture of a mown sward with plenty of clover and the nicer kind of weeds. The point is that some weeds wear out quicker than grass—which is only serious on sports turf, and some weeds damage lawns—Plantains, Dandelions and other rough stuff; but others are just neat little green things which give a velvety look to the grass. Weeds that visibly die in the winter are a nuisance. When doubts come, remember how in Japan they are all busy trying to keep grass out of their beautiful moss lawns! At all events, nowadays the grosser weeds are simple to eradicate with lawn sand weed killers.

In informal, larger gardens, grass can be managed with occasional scything, made easy with machines, and only some areas close mown; the scything can be done after the spring flowers, such as the white Chrysanthemum, have gone.

The Giant Reed (Arundo donax). Many of the reeds, grasses and bamboos have fine form (scale 1/30)

1 and 2 Fatsia japonica and Mahonia
japonica, two plants of strong character
which can stand alone as main
features of even a large garden

3 Vitis Coignetiae, one of the many
splendid large-leaved climbers which
are the best of all plants for giving
an impression of richness to a garden

Trees

Another vast subject. In a small garden one or more large trees may well be already there, and unless they are desperately shading the house, or you are mad about growing some stupid sun-loving plant, it is well to be thankful for such great mercies and plan the whole garden round them. If not, and the sun-loving plants win, never try to reduce the trees by lopping them; cut them down, grub up the roots (that will keep you busy!) and start again.

There is an infinite number of small trees for the garden, but one must choose with care. Many, including some of the prettiest, like the almond, are short lived, and will be dead or decrepit in thirty years. Others, like some Magnolias, take twenty years to produce the first flower and another fifteen to look like they do at Bodnant. In a small garden, it is often better to use the larger shrubs; a large evergreen shrub like Prunus lusitanica, for example, will look more solid and tree-like than many of the smaller trees, which often have a spindly aspect. Trees, like other plants, have been messed about by the plant breeders; and one must guard against falling for some particularly gruesome deformities which are often advertised as suitable for small gardens. One such is Prunus Ama-no-Gawa, a variety of Japanese cherry, which is fastigiate—that is, holds it branches stiffly upwards like a Lombardy Poplar, a sad cripple which casts gloom on many a tiny garden; and all the sadder because of all the trees which weaken's one resolve to do without them in small gardens, the great white and pink Japanese cherries are the loveliest.

Maintenance

For some people the work in a garden is an end in itself. But for most of us, the less work the better. Gone are the days when a small garden meant, to Gertrude Jekyll, one which could be run with one or two gardeners only. Most of us have never seen a gardener, and even those who have will agree that the kind of jobbing gardener available today may do more damage in the garden than a slug of the same size. It is quite easy for even the busiest person to keep a small garden; the key is to plan the garden so that it only takes up the time you have to spare for it. At the minimum, pave the whole thing, have one tree and some climbing plants and do nothing except sweep it occasionally. From there you can go on to have a pot or two, or a bed or two, until you have a truly time-consuming horticultural enterprise on your hands.

Avoid wasting time on unattainable ideals like bowling-green lawns, weedless beds, or the biggest dahlia in the world. Concentrate on having good, well-drained soil. Keep a corner of the garden for a set of compost heaps, on which all garden rubbish goes and any vegetable refuse from the house, and this will keep even town soil in good

Saxifraga cuneifolia forms large cushions of evergreen rosettes: a beautiful, permanenent and trouble free plant (scale ½)

1 Nymphaea alba, the common white waterlily, is as beautiful as any of its hybridised cousins. Note how the beauty of floating plants depends on the lines of light and reflections caused by the leaves bending the surface of the water

2 and 3 Gunnera manicata, at Abbotsbury and Wisley respectively. This is a Chilean plant which likes wet and provides a constantly changing spectacle as its huge leaves grow to 6 ft each year and die away again. At Abbotsbury it grows high enough for you to see the sun coming through the leaves

condition. Plant permanent plants in a plan which will need no drastic change. If you like an informal look about your garden, have a number of favourite weeds, which will seed themselves in odd places. They must be easy to recognise as seedlings, and very easy to pull up, so that when they pop up everywhere you spend an April hour or two decimating them. My favourites are: Papaver somniferum, the Opium Poppy; Corydalis lutea; Meconopsis cambrica, the Welsh Poppy; Verbascum phoenicium; Digitalis purpurea, the Foxglove. I could go on—Impatiens glandulifera, Heracleum mantegazzianium, Angelica archangelica—it just depends how many April afternoons you can spare, and how rough you like it.

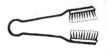

The aphis brush invented by the Rev. F. S. Bull of Colchester. From *The Gardener's Assistant* by Robert Thomson, *c*.1850

Don't worry about *all* weeds; concentrate on getting rid of Goutweed, Bindweed and a few other really hostile plants and live with the rest. Some terrifying weeds—the bulbous-rooted Oxalis for example —seem ineradicable for years and then suddenly give up and leave you. Take the same line with aphids and other insect pests. Sousing the garden with insecticides will do more harm than good; your garden should have a flourishing population of spiders and ladybird beetles and other insect predators fighting on your side; total warfare will lose these allies. Very limited spraying of a few urgent cases—the tips of rose shoots and so on—is all that should be done, and that preferably with an organic insecticide like pyrethrum, derris or nicotine. Even here, a few minutes spent brushing the aphids off *as soon as they appear* with a pair of tooth brushes will do more good, and less harm to the ladybird larvae who can go on and eat any survivors.

Ground-covering plants are a help in suppressing weeds; and they look better than bare soil. Indeed, the aim should be to have no bare soil showing anywhere. The old idea that continuous cultivation of the surface helped the plants, especially shrubs, by conserving moisture is probably mistaken; it almost certainly does not conserve moisture, and does some harm by disturbing shallow roots. Ground-cover plants compete for moisture, but they shade the ground. A mulch, or layer of rotted material such as leaf mould or old manure, is very weed proof and *does* conserve moisture, but it can look disgusting.

Some of my favourite weeds:

1 and 4 The Opium Poppy and the Shirley Poppy would be the best plants in my book if they lasted longer

2 A weedy corner of my garden with Geranium pratense, Geranium robertianum, Astrantia major, Ajuga reptans, etc, competing very pleasantly with a minimum of interference from me

3 Corydalis lutea is a weed, but beautiful and flowers from April until the autumn frosts

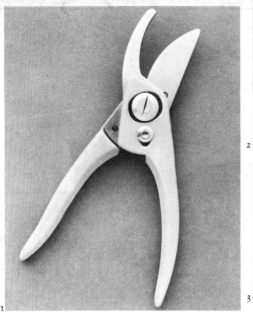

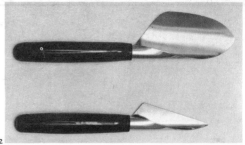

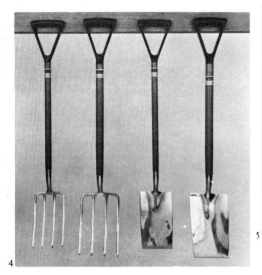

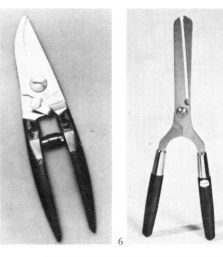

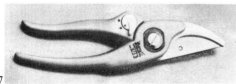

4 Forks and spades. Wilkinson Sword
  (Colnbrook) Ltd
5 Pruner. Wilkinson Sword
  (Colnbrook) Ltd. Model: Compact W55
6 Hand shear. John Guy & Co Ltd.
  Model: 102
7 Pruner. Wilkinson Sword
  (Colnbrook) Ltd. Model: W59
8 Double- and single-bladed knives.
  Wilkinson Sword (Colnbrook) Ltd.
  Models: W150 and W151

1 Pruner. Wilkinson Sword
  (Colnbrook) Ltd. Model: W58
2 "Fine Trowel" and "Fine Point".
  Wilkinson Sword (Colnbrook) Ltd
3 Hand shear. Wilkinson Sword
  (Colnbrook) Ltd. Model: W433